Once upon a time three bears lived in a cottage in the woods. They were Papa Bear, Mama Bear, and Baby Bear.

One morning they decided
to take a walk while their
porridge was cooling.

Soon Goldilocks came to the bears'
cottage. She was lost and hungry.
Since no one was home, she went
right in.

Goldilocks saw three bowls
on the table.
She tasted Papa Bear's porridge.
It was too hot.
She tasted Mama Bear's porridge.
It was too cold.

She tasted Baby Bear's porridge.
It was just right.
So, she ate it all up.

Now Goldilocks wanted to rest.
She saw three chairs.
She sat in the big chair.
It was too hard.
She sat in the middle-sized chair.
It was too soft.

She sat in the little chair.
It was just right.
But, it broke all to pieces.

Goldilocks was very tired.
She saw three beds.
She tried the big bed.
It was too hard.
She tried the middle-sized bed.
It was too soft.

She tried the little bed.
It was just right.
So, she fell fast asleep.

The three bears came back.
Papa Bear said, "Someone
has been eating my porridge."
Mama bear said, "Someone
has been eating my porridge."

Baby Bear said, "Someone
has been eating my porridge.
And, they ate it all up!"

The bears saw their chairs.
Papa Bear said, "Someone
has been sitting in my chair."
Mama Bear said, "Someone
has been sitting in my chair."

Baby Bear said, "Someone
has been sitting in my chair.
And, it is all broken."

The three bears saw their beds.
Papa Bear said, "Someone
has been sleeping in my bed."
Mama bear said, "Someone
has been sleeping in my bed."

Baby Bear said, "Someone
has been sleeping in my bed.
And, here she is!"

Goldilocks woke up. When she
saw the three bears, she jumped
out of bed and ran home.